MEMOS

MEMOS

Susan Terris

OMNIDAWN PUBLISHING
RICHMOND, CALIFORNIA
2015

Cover image: Autobiography #13 by Diane Rosenblum
courtesy of the artist.

Cover and interior design by Peter Burghardt

Typefaces: Palatino Linotype and Centaur MT Standard.

Offset printed in the United States
by Edwards Brothers Malloy, Ann Arbor, Michigan
On 55# Glatfelter B18 Antique
Acid Free Archival Quality Recycled Paper
with Rainbow FSC Certified Colored End Papers

Published by Omnidawn Publishing, Richmond, California
www.omnidawn.com   (510) 237-5472   (800) 792-4957
10 9 8 7 6 5 4 3 2 1
ISBN: 978-1-63243-006-9

-Contents-

MEMO TO THE WILD GIRL I WAS

back then   baby   you prowled half-built houses
fell through thin ice on the pond   went to jazz

joints   oh St. Louie Woman   in East St. L   you
sole underage listener with a white face

lone cyclist pedaling out Highway 40   your fort
in the wooded tract   next to the projects

copperhead you tried to tame   no diamond rings
but   hey   you lived to see the evening sun go down

MEMO TO SELF

as the tiger is your daemon   Molly Bloom and
the Wife of Bath are your companions   your BFFs

women after love and sex   freedom and license
women who say *yes*

Memo to the Man Who Gave Me His Mother's Wedding Ring

by mistake   after all the times   like Emma Bovary
I'd begged for one   there in the bottom of

the suede pouch with the heishi   gift for my birthday
that gold ring with an arc of rose-cut diamonds

a thirties kind of piece   older than you think   maybe
your mother's mother's and yet   for five months

mine   too small for my fingers though   not mine after all
each stone sharp enough to cut glass

Memo to the Homeless Woman by the Sutter Stockton Garage

the cardboard sign says   I'm hungry   says   AIDS
stained hoodie   market cart and pooch with pointed ears

why you instead of me   who gave me Rosie to ride
and you only old tickets torn in half

I say   stop   I want to get off   while you keep
trying to get on   around and around   I try not to eye

you   sitting cross-legged   head bowed   I throw
money   can't bear the month-old baby in your lap

Memo to the Girl in the Body of a Boy

if bone and bone were split   if hair didn't grow
the nightlight might burn out   if marbles

spin outside their circles   girl-brother
boy-sister   this road is indifferently paved

contralto cries and a Beethoven sonata
skin-deep is deep skin   not just one more bruise

Memo to the Boys in Pajamas at Starbucks on Sunday Morning

you there in Gap pajamas   toddler   infant   father
a raisin bagel and two plain   you reel me back decades

to Fantasia   a phantom now   razed for office space
my child always picked butterhorns   the biggest

baked by Ernie Weil   Fantasia   not *Bald Mountain*
or *Sorcerer*   just delicate sweet pastries

and the trek to buy them   mythic   lighter than bagels
yet you boys in Starbucks   own a newer myth

MEMO TO THE GIRL WITH THE PORT-WINE STAIN ACROSS HER FACE

a teenager   you're standing in front of the Lincoln Memorial
place which declares all created equal   and your friends

are photographing you   not profile so only the unblemished
shows   but full face and smiling   audacious even

your parents   I'd like to know them   people who love
a girl with dreams of her own   girl   who lives unmarked

Memo to the Deadbeat Dad

think about the no-garden garden   how rain falls
on untilled ground   no spade and no hoe

or shovel of black dirt with earthworms   the checks
the balances   no matter what you plant   rhubarb

and zucchini will triumph   today or tomorrow
no sticky fingers stuck to yours   no green snot

overseas   earthquake and tsunami   and here
young unseen shoots   tender   untended

Memo to the Boys of West Virginia

mountaintop removal   boom   geologic plunder
next to a school   toxic sludge pond

dynamite   catfish streams and piney woods gone
big coal moves all   dynamite   boys whose

fathers mine   will be   dynamite   miners too
bread for the company   bread for your tables

mountaintop reclamation   a moonscape joke
yet poison   fire   dynamite   you need those booms

Memo to the Man Whose Dog Died

blond hairs still bond to trousers   and in the garage
leashes still hang   the rubber bone you threw

missing   unconditional love   folks you met
out dogging   a warm body in bed   once when

when you crayoned everyone's dogs waiting at
the Pearly Gates   a teacher said dogs had

no souls   but now   soulful   you call out in
sleep   and dig up the dead   growl   roll

Memo to the Guy Who Thinks It's Funny When I Talk Sports

yes   in the red zone   or a tomato can   and lay-ups
I said   double-teamed   foul balls   icing the puck

or being again offsides   to punt or go for it   to bunt
or be a switch-hitter swinging for the fences   hah

you asked me what a tight end does   about love-love
so I told you   firmly   I have a pencil and keep score

Memo to Self

you're more like the Emmas   Bovary and Woodhouse
rash and wrong-headed and brooking no opposition

more like Kitty than Elizabeth Bennet   or like Tess
and Eustacia   double-double toil   trouble

MEMO TO THE WAITER AT ABSINTHE

snake tattoo and a buttery voice   another actor
waiting for call-backs   a quick study   you

tick through daily specials   including crab in
black bean sauce with fennel and kelp   take orders

dressing on the side   and leek soup without cream
hold the cilantro   to be or not to be   not the tips

that get you through the night   but the questions
the fardels   the bare bodkin   lines   the break

Memo to the Young Streetwalker

I can still see the soft spot   your parchment
head cradled   your once-upon-a-timeness

was it a rabbit or doll you slept with
did someone beat   or fondle

or were you   instead   a bright unruly kite
who snapped its twine and lost its tail

Memo to the NRA

if I tell you I need an assault rifle
to explode watermelons   would I be sane

or would I be one more whackjob who should be
locked up   sure   brandish that amendment

but guns do kill   people walking down the street
people in a corner store   school children

if I'd had a pistol when I found a burglar ten feet
from where my children slept   I would have

tried to kill him   but he   young and scared
might have taken both it   and me

Memo to the Former Child Prodigy

by the age of nine   you knew everything   tra-la
French and Latin   *tra-la*   could explain pi

memorize *The Mikado*   Shakespeare soliloquies
or checkmate anyone blind-folded   child's play

violin   oboe   harpsichord   duplicate bridge
so what   then   was left to do

cut corners   fit in   marry someone
polish silver   slap your children   or go back

back to one   *tra-la*   then two and so forth
'til you learn to love what blooms *in the spring*

Memo to the Woman Who Thinks You Can't Be Too Rich or Too Thin

the coda you added to rich and thin was white blouses
one could never have too many   you said   then

the daughter who tried to starve herself into submission
changed my mind about thin   and old ladies   I've noticed

come either too thin or too fat   one a-penny two a-penny
money its own story   coins for the ferryman may be
required

but happy has no price tag   and thin is better for watches
or pancakes   though you may be right about white blouses

Memo to the Man Who's Romancing A Girl Less Than Half His Age

even your best friends won't tell you of the sex toys
she ordered   and bragged about on Facebook   nor will

they share with you the joke about the Sleep Number Bed
where they know she's a 27   while you're a 68

Memo to My House Plants

listen up   spathiphyllum   phaelaenopsis
and ficus   you are here on sufferance

like all guests   time limits apply   tick-tock
demand too much care and coddling

expulsion will follow   you are like streetcars
blossom for your keep before others come by

rooting for a home   grow   or the recycle truck
will snap its maw and chew you to compost

Memo to My Husband

when we married I was so young and stupid
I could not have known   that everything I wanted

to do   you'd say   yes   we'll find a way   freedom
granted freely

MEMO TO THE LITTLE GIRL IN THE TUTU AND FROGGIE RAIN BOOTS

no curl in the middle of your forehead   just a need
to stomp one foot   and a voice that projects

don't tell me you stepped in dog shit   and that's
why you're in frog boots on a day with no rain

indeed   an individualist already   baby woman
and clear-sighted as my granddaughter who

in Disneyland   didn't dress like a princess   but
as Minnie Mouse   stiff blunt-toed shoes and all

MEMO TO SELF

how could you have forgotten Heathcliff   but you
have   after decades of ache and lust   if he

were to gallop off the moors now   you'd probably bitch
he needs more than a shower and a shave

Memo to the N. J. Poet Who Bet Me the Super Bowl Spread

when I was growing up spread meant   Miracle Whip
you put on Wonder Bread with the baloney

what legs did in cement boots   in the Mississippi
if you piqued the St. Louis Mafia

what you put on top of scratchy wool blankets after
you squared hospital corners   and we never

said *point spread* but *odds*   not on games but horses
running at Hialeah   and spread was also what

other girls' mothers said not to do before marriage

Memo to My Twin Polar Star

yes   we explore dark matter   and dark loins
which Lawrence found so compelling   or consider

Marvell's wingéd chariot   but space is empty
pathetic fallacies abound   poetry only

muddles the issues   how many light years
when there is not world enough   love   or time

Memo to the Editor Who Keeps Rejecting My Work

my good friend says acceptance from your journal
comes only   if a poet accumulates enough shine

look   I'm dancing as fast as I can   but even if I were
to strip   I know you're saying   *don't*   I'm not

the 30 year old phenom   though she's very thin and
you might not want her naked either   but you and I

have a deal   once each October   waltz not tango
then your note   nice work   sorry   try me next year

Memo to the Widow Who's Still Grieving

you're supposed to suck it up   the old plaid
bathrobe   rusting lawnmower   letters found from

another woman   but what of the canoe you two
tipped in the wild rice   how dying he told you

your price was above rubies   north-by-northwest
is the way to distress not healing   but mourning

at morning   to pack him in boxes and move him to
the attic   may only send a mad woman there

Memo to the Woman in Deep Denial

beware all who enter here   not your mother's
Alzheimer's or your father's heart attacks

but at the Indian buffet   and then on the sidewalk
glioblastoma   if you think you have to ask   don't

you talk   instead   of Chinese women's little lilies
why Walden is a pond not a lake   how

the King Charles yap dog riles up allergies
and how   these days   denial's the only safe place

flip a coin and find   like in a Stoppard play
all time suspended so it's heads   heads   heads

Memo to Self

when you were Kitty's age and first met Anna K
you thought   to die for love was fierce   brave   yet by

forty   you knew   if you'd loved not Vronsky but Levin
you'd still be dead

Memo to the Volunteers at Fukushima

you stayed   yes   *the forest owl said*   you
stayed   to save the air   the others

but the babies   who can save   delicate
eyes and arms   *wolves and kitsune won't come near*

their ten fingers   ten toes   *sleep*   don't count
the babies   *sleep*   the water and winds   *gorosuke*

hoo hoo   the blue tsunami   oh the babies
too soon   a wave will come   *gorosuke hoo*

Memo to My Sister-in-Law the Day Before She Dies

stage four   hairless bed of bones   remember how
gorgeous you were   only months ago at the museum

now thin is excruciating   why the chemo won't help
and your fierce old lover's back to nurse you

Irish guilt perhaps   let us go now to Innisfree
all the perfections useless   cherrywood closets

emerald necklace your husband never knew of
you grip me with ghost fingers   say clay and

wattles   say you don't know what's happening   say
do something   I tell them you want more morphine

Memo to the Names I Can't Remove from My Address Book

Mother's still here and Bob   Ann stays in the "R"s with
Claude and Louise and Mort   near Ted in the "T"s

my husband always now predicting his own death
insists the dead are forgotten   how often his mother

returns to speak   I don't tell him   if I erase   you
the dead   will you claw back at me   grieving for

your losses as well as mine   Charon wants the coin
placed on his tongue   but have we gone through

his pockets for the days in Sedona or Easthampton
nights in New Orleans and San Mateo and Banff

I beg Dark-Hood   to give them back   and ye who enter
don't give up   we are not yet done

Memo to My Children

since I've already written the poem about pearls
wet boots and windfall   and I prize you

I can only say   *kinehora*
for your successes   I take no credit

and for your failures   best beloveds   listen
it's all right to fail   I do too

Memo to the Lake House in Park Rapids, Minnesota

neither distance nor knots of time can fray
ties   my paddle's keen and bright   lake dipping

mother and father   children we were and are
the grandparents and newer children   you hold

us all   days flash with silver   ashes   nights your
wooden ribs creak   as you breathe out   and then in

first love   best love   you're mine   your sunshine
your thundering   ashes   your fresh pine smell

MEMO TO SELF

neither Beatrice nor Laura   you are
no one's muse   no poet extolls your virtues

invokes immortality   but still you may a-
muse and intimate immoralilty

Memo to the Cat Who Keeps Bringing Me Half-Dead Birds

tremor of wounded breast   twitch of wing remembering
for these gifts   Grimalkin   I do not thank you

love comes in many forms   the almost moribund I know
too well   so stop reminding me   fangs are everywhere

ding-dong-bell   my own heart pierced often by words
or by neglect   like it or not   stop   we're all mad here

Memo to the Man Who's Losing His Mind

accumulations drift   knick knack paddy whack
you're more obsessive now   dog and his bone

once your mother   the nurse   said she felt
someone with a washrag   scrubbing her brain

away   your notes help   but seem to copy themselves
at night   multiply like empty hangers in a closet

and   old man   you play one   and then again one
no matter how hard you try   fear breeds caution

words cyclone   blow chill winds through
you   I love   but you play knick knack on my spine

Memo to My Friend Who Does Outrage for Us All

earthquakes   gas mains   fires   tsunamis
homeless women on the street   the 49ers

writers whose novels end lamely   Fox News
martinis not bruised   Yemen   Pakistan

cars that block driveways   men who cheat
nepotism at city hall   and the state capitol

women who talk only about clothes   or houses
pirates   misplaced sentiment   plastic

Tibet   circus animals   Korea   the Tenderloin
guns   clean water   bedbugs   elections

oh   you're outrage central   you worry
so we don't   etcetera etcetera   and so forth

Memo to the Woman Who Wants to Run Away

spell out the reasons as if talking with Helen Keller
is the distance near or far   can you walk it in a week

sing a song of sixpence   and of a no-life life
ask yourself if it's too late   and how long

you'd have to hide   and about the job of just enough
sweaters folded   footsteps only your own

pansies in the window box   plate   bowl   spoon
scissors in every drawer   the newest *Anna Karenina*

only one lock on the door   but two keys
the soothing order of disorder and of disambiguation

MEMO TO SELF

some days you're Jane   waiting for Mr. Rochester
to see the fire beyond the plain brown wood of you

but also   the madwoman upstairs   raging
as both of you tinder the flames

ACKNOWLEDGMENTS

Many of the poems from *MEMOS*, some in slightly different versions, have appeared in the following publications:

Barrow Street, Blue Fifth, California Quarterly, Denver Quarterly, Great River Review, Main Street Rag, Many Mountains Moving, Passages North, Poetrybay, Poetry Congeries (Connotation Press), and *Talking Writing.*

The poem "Memo to the Former Child Prodigy," which was published in the *Denver Quarterly,* has been selected for *The Best American Poetry 2015,* guest editor Sherman Alexie, series editor David Lehman.

 Susan Terris' poetry books include *Ghost of Yesterday: New & Selected Poems, The Homelessness of Self, Contrariwise, Natural Defenses, Fire is Favorable to the Dreamer, Poetic License,* and *Eye of the Holocaust.* Her work has appeared in many publications including: *Colorado Review, Denver Quarterly, The Iowa Review, FIELD, The Journal, Prairie Schooner, The Southern Review, Volt,* and *Ploughshares.* For seven years, with CB Follett, she edited *RUNES, A Review Of Poetry.* She is now editor of *Spillway* and a poetry editor for *Pedestal Magazine* and *In Posse Review.* She had a poem from *FIELD* published in *PUSHCART PRIZE XXXI.*